366 **DAYS**

※

OF WISDOM

&

INSPIRATION

※

with
America's Success Coach

Tommy Newberry
Author of *Success Is Not An Accident*

MASON PRESS

Mason Press
Atlanta, Georgia

Copyright © 1997 Tommy Newberry

All rights reserved, including the right to reproduce this book or portions thereof in any form whatsoever.

Manufactured in the United States of America

Library of Congress Cataloging Card Number 96-95187

ISBN 1-886669-08-2

America's Success Coach and The 1% Club are registered trademarks of Tommy Newberry Coaching Systems, Inc.

ALSO BY TOMMY NEWBERRY

Success Is Not An Accident

Getting Results

High Speed Success

Vital Time

Talk Yourself Into Success

Peak Performance For Christ

For additional copies of
366 Days of Wisdom and Inspiration
call
800-643-9770
or
404-237-6859

This book is dedicated
to the members of The 1% Club®
for their unique resolve
and active commitment
to maximize their God-given potential
in all areas of life.

I am truly blessed to be your coach.
Your high character, high performance,
high impact example
touches more lives than you realize.
I have gained much wisdom and inspiration
from each and every one of you.

Continue to Think Huge!
Tommy

FOREWORD

For years I have collected the better thoughts and observations of some of history's wisest thinkers, writers and doers. I have noticed that high achievers in all walks of life have an unquenchable thirst for ideas, insights and inspiration. The energizing and encouraging power of the *right thoughts* is fascinating to witness. Right thoughts are thoughts anchored in timeless truth. They are thoughts that promote self-reliance, integrity, commitment, individual responsibility, accountability, faith, perseverance, and personal excellence. These qualities are, for the most part, learned. They bring out the best in an individual and, when undiluted, allow a society to develop its full potential.

I have often been asked to share the quotations I have collected with others. This book is an attempt to do just that. I believe that wisdom is the perfect blend of experience and reflection. Invest the time to be still and dwell upon the time-tested truths in the pages that follow. Remember, whatever you think about over and over becomes part of your character. This book is intended to be a constant companion and coach, providing you with a steady stream of positive mental nutrition. Refer to it often and share its ideas with those you love.

Successfully and Positively,
Tommy Newberry

DAY 1

Success is not an accident.

Tommy Newberry

Don't join an easy crowd.
You won't grow.
Go where the expectations and
the demands to perform are high.

Jim Rohn

DAY 2

Mind is the master power that moulds and makes,
And man is mind, and evermore he takes
The tool of thought, and, shaping what he wills,
Brings forth a thousand joys, a thousand ills:
He thinks in secret, and it comes to pass:
Environment is but his looking glass.

James Allen

It sometimes seems that intense desire
creates not only its own opportunities,
but its own talents.

Eric Hoffer

Little minds attain and
are subdued by misfortune;
but great minds rise above them.

Washington Irving

Day 3

Life is no brief candle to me.
It is a sort of splendid torch which
I have got hold of for the moment,
and I want to make it burn as brightly as possible
before handing it on to future generations.

George Bernard Shaw

Progress in any activity is made
only when its potentiality is envisioned,
not when it is restricted by reality.

David Schwartz

Day 4

He has achieved success who has lived well,
laughed often, and loved much.

Day 5

Successful people come in all ages, shapes, sizes and colors. But they have one thing in common: a winning attitude

Earl Nightingale

You can't reach your goals without occasionally taking some long shots.

Day 6

Mastery just doesn't come without deliberate repetitive practice and a constant desire for never-ending advancement and improvement.

Tommy Newberry

The world is not interested in the storms you encountered, but whether you brought in the ship.

Journal of True Education

Day 7

If one advances confidently in the direction of his dreams, and endeavors to live the life which he has imagined, he will meet with success unexpected in common hours.

Henry David Thoreau

Day 8

Every winner has scars.

Herbert N. Casson

One: Success is not designed to be easy.
Two: Success is based on failure.
Three: The only difference between a failure and a success is that the success decides to get up one more time.

Burgess Owens

Day 9

Goals are what make us stretch.
They cause us to move out of
our comfort zone and operate on the outer
edge of our potential as human beings,
so make your goals challenging.

Brian Tracy

People are changed,
not by coercion or intimidation,
but by example.

John Maxwell

Day 10

Success is never final.
Failure is never fatal.
It's courage that counts.

Sam Rutigliano

Courage is rightly considered
the foremost of the virtues
for upon it all others depend.

Winston Churchill

Day 11

For everyone to whom much is given, from him much will be required.

Luke 12:48

Formal education will make you a living. Self-education will make you a fortune.

Jim Rohn

Day 12

No statue was ever erected to the memory of a person who thought it best to leave well enough alone.

Joey Reiman

While faith makes all things possible, it is love that makes all things easy.

DAY 13

Most negative stress
comes from underachieving,
from doing less than you know
you're capable of doing.

Tommy Newberry

Champions are made by risking more than
others think is safe,
dreaming more than others think is practical,
and expecting more than others think is possible.

Jack Nicklaus

DAY 14

People with character are always seeking
new ways to grow their skills
and develop their talents.

They want to be better tomorrow
than they are today.

They are never satisfied
with resting on past accomplishments
and maintaining the status quo.
Growth is the goal.

Day 15

It is better to light one wee candle,
than to curse the darkness.

Scottish Proverb

There's an original song inside you – *sing it!*
If it seems like a strange little song,
sing often – it will soon catch on – but *sing it!*
"Alas, for those who never sing,
but die with all their music in them."

Day 16

You have to believe in yourself.
And you have to, down
deep within the bottom of your soul,
feel that you can
do the job that you've set out to do.

William Castle DeVries

Thought is action in rehearsal.

Sigmund Freud

You can do what you want to do.
You can be what you want to be.

R. David Thomas

DAY 17

Keep your heart with all diligence,
for out of it spring the issues of life.

Proverbs 4:23

We develop opportunity by
applying persistence to the possibilities.
Opportunity is all around us.
If we seek it, we will find it.
And if the door of opportunity is closed,
we must knock on it.
and keep on knocking until it opens.

DAY 18

Underachievers don't fail more,
they're just more afraid of failing.

Tommy Newberry

DAY 19

Example teaches better than precept.
It is the best molder of the character of
men and women.
To set a lofty example is the richest bequest a
man can leave behind.

Samuel Smiles

DAY 20

Yesterday is only a dream
and tomorrow
but a vision…
yet each day well lived
makes every yesterday
a dream of happiness,
and each tomorrow, a vision of hope.
Look well, therefore,
to this one day,
for it alone is life.

Day 21

You can decide within yourself
how circumstances will affect you.
Between what happens to you,
or the stimulus, and your response to it,
is your freedom or power
to choose that response.

Stephen Covey

It is not enough to have a good mind.
The main thing is to use it well.

Rene Descartes

Day 22

Adapt an extended, long-term perspective.
You excel in life to the extent that
you apply a long-term perspective in making
your most important decisions.

Tommy Newberry

The food that enters the mind
must be watched as closely as
the food that enters the body.

Patrick Buchanan

Now faith is the substance of things hoped for, the evidence of things not seen.

Hebrews 11:1

Day 23

Man is the only animal that laughs and weeps, for he is the only animal that is struck with the difference between what things are, and what they ought to be.

William Hazlitt

How badly do you want it?

George Allen

Day 24

Do you see a man skilled in his work? I tell you he will stand before kings; he will not stand before obscure men.

Proverbs 22:29

What matters is not the size of the
dog in the fight,
but the size of the fight in the dog.

Bear Bryant

DAY 25

The battle of life is, in most cases, fought uphill;
and to win it without a struggle
were perhaps to win it without honour. If there
were no difficulties there would be
no success; if there were nothing to struggle for,
there would be nothing to be achieved.

Practice believing that God is as real and actual
as your wife, or your business partner,
or your closest friend.
Practice talking matters over with Him;
believe that He hears and gives thought
to your problem.

Norman Vincent Peale

DAY 26

Laughter is inner jogging.

Norman Cousins

The courage to finally take one's life in one's
own hands and go after the big dream
has a way of making dreams come true.

Earl Nightingale

Day 27

There is always enough time to get
those things done
that God wants you to do!

Jim Collins

Whatever you seem to enjoy the most
is a very good indication
of where your strengths lie.

Brian Tracy

Day 28

You will never win if you never begin.

Robert Schuller

> Finally, brethren,
> whatever is true,
> whatever is honorable,
> whatever is just,
> whatever is pure,
> whatever is lovely,
> whatever is gracious,
> if there is any excellence,
> if there is anything worthy of praise,
> think about these things!
>
> *Philippians 4:8*

Day 29

> The people you habitually associate with are
> like the buttons on an elevator.
> They'll either take you up or down.
>
> *Tommy Newberry*

> Three things are to be looked to in a building:
> that it stand on the right spot;
> that it be securely founded;
> that it be successfully executed.
>
> *Goethe*

Day 30

Day 31

Treasure the love you receive
above all. It will survive long after
your gold and good health have vanished.

Og Mandino

Day 32

You are equal to all others.
Some may have greater talents and power
where you are lacking,
but you are greater in areas where they cannot go.
Do not stop your own growth and progression
by trying to emulate or follow anyone.
Step out with courage.

Develop all that you are meant to be;
Look for new experiences, meet new people,
learn to add all new dimensions
to your present and future.
You are one of a kind equal to every other person.
Accept that fact.
Live it, use it, stand tall in belief of who you are.
Reach for the highest accomplishment.
Touch it. Grasp it.
Know it is within your ability.
Live to win in life and you will.

Diane Westlake

Procrastination and worry are the twin thieves
that will try to rob you of your brilliance –
but even the smallest action drives them from
your camp.

Gil Atkinson

DAY
33

The man who follows the crowd will never be
followed by a crowd.

Talent develops in quiet places, character in the
full current of human life.

Goethe

A hundred years from now it will not matter
what my bank account was,
the sort of house I lived in,
or the kind of car I drove…
But the world may be different because
I was important in the life of a child.

DAY
34

Day 35

As one successful parent said about
raising children,
"Treat them all the same by treating
them differently,"
respecting their differences.

Stephen Covey

If you are not making the progress
that you would like to make
and are capable of making,
it is because your goals are not clearly defined.

Paul J. Meyer

I'd rather fail than be mediocre!

Tommy Newberry

Day 36

Compared with what we ought to be, we are
only half awake.
Our fires are damped, our drafts are checked.
We are making use of only a small part
of our possible mental and physical resources.

William James

Day 37

Ask, and it will be given to you; seek, and you will find; knock, and it will be opened unto you. For every one who asks receives; and he who seeks finds; and to him who knocks it shall be opened.

Matthew 7:7-8

Character Counts.
And little else matters in the absence of it.

Tommy Newberry

Day 38

It's the job that's never started that takes longest to finish.

J.R.R. Tolkien

Other people's views and troubles can be contagious. Don't sabotage yourself by unwittingly adopting negative, unproductive attitudes through your associations with others.

Epictetus

Remember that while the doctor treats you,
God heals you.

Norman Vincent Peale

Day 39

Every now and then go away, even briefly, have a little relaxation, for when you come back to your work your judgment will be surer; since to remain constantly at work will cause you to lose power...

Leonardo da Vinci

Faith is to believe
what you do not yet see;
the reward for this faith
is to see what you believe.

St. Augustine

Day 40

Repeat anything often enough
and it will start to become you.

Tom Hopkins

A man is known
by the company his mind keeps.

Thomas Bailey Aldrich

DAY 41

The fight is won or lost far away from witnesses–
behind the lines, in the gym
and out there on the road,
long before I dance under those lights.

Muhammad Ali

The point is this; he who sows sparingly
will also reap sparingly;
and he who sows bountifully
will also reap bountifully.

2 Corinthians 9:6

DAY 42

The world is moving so fast these days that
the man who says it can't be done
is generally interrupted by someone doing it.

Harry Emerson Fosdick

Day 43

If you want your mission in life to become a magnificent obsession,
you have to constantly remind yourself
of that mission.

Tommy Newberry

My father taught that the only helping hand
you're ever going to be able to rely on
is the one at the end of your sleeve.

J.C. Watts

Day 44

A man can only rise, conquer,
and achieve by lifting up his thoughts.

James Allen

Habit is habit, and not to be flung
out of the window,
but coaxed downstairs a step at a time.

Mark Twain

W hat you do not wish others
should do unto you,
do not so do unto them.

Confucius

I start where the last man left off.

Thomas Edison

DAY 45

Y ou have to decide what your
highest priorities are
and have the courage... pleasantly, smilingly,
apologetically... to say "no" to other things.
And the way you do that is by having
a bigger "yes" burning inside.
The enemy of the "best" is often the "good."

Stephen Covey

C ommon sense is not so common.

Voltaire

DAY 46

Don't get married for better or for worse; get married for better and better.

Mark Victor Hansen

Day 47

The greatest gift you can give to somebody is your own personal development.
I used to say, "If you will take care of me, I will take care of you."
Now I say, "I will take care of me for you, if you will take care of you for me."

Jim Rohn

Intuitive feelings always guide you in a direction of growth and purposefulness.

Wayne Dyer

Day 48

Losers fix the blame, winners fix the situation.
Losers say "Why don't *they* do something?"
Winners say, "Here's something *I* can do."

Day 49

The significant problems we face cannot be
solved at the same level
of thinking we were at when we created them.

Albert Einstein

A noble person attracts noble people,
and knows how to hold on to them.

Goethe

Day 50

It is not best to swap horses while
crossing the river.

Abraham Lincoln

Nothing great is created suddenly,
any more than a bunch of grapes or a fig.
If you tell me that you desire a fig,
I answer you that there must be time.
Let it first blossom, then bear fruit, then ripen.

Epictetus

You'll get old and gray waiting around for the impulse to create change in your life.
So don't wait for the feeling, stand up and make the decision to do it right now.

Tommy Newberry

Day 51

No matter what your aims or resolutions or professions may be,
it is by your deeds that you are judged.

Henry Ward Beecher

Some men see things as they are and say, "Why?"
I dream things that never were and say, "Why not?"

George Bernard Shaw

Obstacles are the raw materials
of great accomplishment.

Tommy Newberry

Day 52

In the middle of difficulty lies opportunity.

Albert Einstein

If you are pained by an external thing
it is not the thing that disturbs you,
but your own judgment about it,
and it is in your power
to wipe out this judgment now.

Marcus Aurelius

DAY 53

Whatever the struggle
continue the climb,
it may be only
one step to the summit.

Diane Westlake

Love is the immortal flow of energy
that nourishes, extends and preserves.
Its eternal goal is life.

Smiley Blanton

DAY 54

Day 55

It is my right to be uncommon – if I can.
I seek opportunity – not security.
I want to take the calculated risk;
to dream and to build, to fail and to succeed.
I refuse to barter incentive for a dole.
I prefer the challenges of life to the guaranteed existence: the thrill of fulfillment to the stale calm of utopia.
I will not trade freedom for beneficence nor my dignity for a handout.
I will never cower before any master nor bend to any threat.

It is my heritage to stand erect, proud and unafraid; to think and act for myself, enjoy the benefit of my creations and to face the world boldly and say, this I have done. All this is what it means to be an American.

Dean Alfange

Day 56

Treat a man as he is and he will remain as he is.
Treat a man as he can and should be and
he will become as he can and should be.

Goethe

DAY 57

If you want to know what you sowed in the past look around you and notice what you're reaping today.

Tommy Newberry

All our dreams can come true... if we have the courage to pursue them.

Walt Disney

DAY 58

Aerodynamically the bumblebee shouldn't be able to fly, but the bumblebee doesn't know it, so it goes on flying anyway.

Mary Kay Ash

Get involved with work that is bigger than yourself, and you'll attract energy and vitality that you never knew was available.

Tommy Newberry

Pay now, play later;
play now, pay later.

John Maxwell

Day 59

The wise don't tell everything they know,
but the foolish talk too much and are ruined.

Proverbs 10:14

Obstacles are those frightful things you see
when you take your eyes off your goals.

Harmony is one phase of the great law
whose spiritual expression is love.

James Allen

Day 60

Nature has so built man that he has absolute
control over the material that reaches his
subconscious mind through his five senses,
although this is not meant to be
construed as a statement that man always
exercises this control.

Napoleon Hill

If a man has done his best,
what else is there?

George Patton

Everything can be taken away from a man
but one thing:
the last of the human freedoms –
to choose one's attitude in any given set of
circumstances, to choose one's own way.

Viktor E. Frankl

DAY 61

Meticulous planning will enable everything a
man does to appear spontaneous.

Mark Caine

We put career, money and pleasure all ahead of
family. The irony is, if we put family first,
the rest will tend to follow a lot more readily.

Harvey Mackay

DAY 62

Day 63

Do all things with love.

Og Mandino

Those who have never finished a big race can tell you all the reasons why you shouldn't enter yours. Don't listen to them!

Day 64

You must be willing to be a little uncomfortable or uneasy if you want the rewards of higher levels of personal effectiveness.

Tommy Newberry

The difference between the impossible and the possible lies in our determination.

Tommy Lasorda

Day 65

The master in the art of living makes little distinction between his work and his play, his labor and his leisure, his mind and his body, his information and his recreation, his love and his religion. He hardly knows which is which. He simply pursues his vision of excellence at whatever he does, leaving others to decide whether he is working or playing.
To him he's always doing both.

James Michener

Day 66

Nothing is more noble,
nothing more venerable than fidelity.
Faithfulness and truth are the most sacred
excellences and endowments of the human mind.

Cicero

Every good thought you think is contributing it's share to the ultimate result of your life.

Grenville Kleiser

Day 67

We are engineered as goal seeking mechanisms.
We are built that way.
When we have no personal goal which we are
interested in and which "means something" to us,
we are apt to "go around in circles,"
feel "lost" and find life itself "aimless."
People who say that life is not worthwhile are
really saying that they themselves have no
personal goals which are worthwhile.

Maxwell Maltz

Day 68

More gold has been mined from the thoughts of man than has ever been taken from the earth.

Napoleon Hill

The heights by great men reached and kept
were not attained by sudden flight,
but they, while their companions slept,
were toiling upward in the night.

Henry Wadsworth Longfellow

DAY 69

Good thoughts and actions can never produce bad results;
bad thoughts and actions can never produce good results.

James Allen

Attitude will make or break a leader.

John Maxwell

DAY 70

Problems are only opportunities with work clothes.

Harry J. Kaiser

Discovery is seeing what everybody else has seen,
and thinking what nobody else has thought.

Albert Szent-Gyorgi

Day 71

Honesty is the first chapter in the book of wisdom.

Thomas Jefferson

The creative minority who do are the envy of the masses who stand by and just watch.

Tommy Newberry

Day 72

Many people say things to themselves that they would never, ever say to a respected friend.
Be a respected friend to yourself.
Be a nourishing friend to yourself.

Tommy Newberry

We make a living by what we get, and a life by what we give.

Winston Churchill

DAY 73

Faith is the confidence,
the assurance,
the enforcing truth,
the knowing......

Robert Collier

According to the depth from which
you draw your life,
such is the depth of your accomplishment.

Ralph Waldo Emerson

DAY 74

If you don't know
where you are going,
how can you expect to get there?

Basil S. Walsh

First you make your habits, then your
habits make you.

John Dryden

Day 75

Love is the most important
ingredient to success.
Without it, our life echoes emptiness.
With it, our life vibrates warmth and meaning.
Even in hardship, love shines through.
Therefore, search for love.
Once we have learned to love, we
will have learned to live.

The race is not always to the swift,
but to those who keep on running.

Day 76

The indisposable first step to getting the things
you want out of life is this; decide what you want.

Ben Stein

The only honest measure of your success
is what you are doing compared to your
true potential.

Paul J. Meyer

When you're ready for a thing, it will make its appearance.

Napoleon Hill

God knows a wonderful and joyous solution to any problem, dilemma, or crises. Ask Him!

Tommy Newberry

DAY 77

The secret of living a life of excellence is merely a matter of thinking thoughts of excellence.
Really, it's a matter of programming our minds with the kind of information that will set us free.

Charles Swindoll

DAY 78

Day 79

As water is to flowers... so is praise to the heart of man. We thrive on being appreciated, loved and needed. When we make others feel important, and show them respect and praise, they do their best. Nothing stimulates growth so much as praise. Whatever we praise we increase.

Remember you will not always win. Some days, the most resourceful individual will taste defeat but there is, in this case, always tomorrow – after you have done your best to achieve success today.

Maxwell Maltz

Day 80

Accept the challenges so that you may feel the exhilaration of victory.

George S. Patton

L̲ove... force it and it disappears.
You cannot will love, nor even control it.
You can only guide its expression.
It comes or it goes according to those qualities
in life that invite it or deny its presence.

David Seabury

DAY 81

Never let what you cannot do interfere
with what you can do.

John Wooden

Procrastination is all about excuses, and you
know as well as I do that the excuses you have
today are the excuses you will have tomorrow.
Today's excuses are but the ancestors to
tomorrow's excuses and the predecessors
to future mediocrity.

Tommy Newberry

DAY 82

Day 83

No man ever achieved worthwhile success who did not, at one time or other, find himself with at least one foot hanging well over the brink of failure.

Napoleon Hill

God is as large as you allow Him to be. He is also as small as you confine Him to be.

Paul Yonggi Cho

Day 84

The only place where success comes before work is a dictionary.

Vidal Sassoon

Blessed is he who has learned to laugh at himself, for he shall never cease to be entertained.

John Powell

Praise invariably implies a reference
to a higher standard.

Aristotle

DAY 85

As you grow older, you'll find the only things
you regret are the things you didn't do.

Zachary Scott

Look at your natural river. Don't you see
there is no effort if you are
riding with your river?

Carl Frederick

DAY 86

Argue for your limitations,
and sure enough, they're yours!

Richard Bach

Day 87

Love is a canvas furnished by Nature
and embroidered by imagination.

Voltaire

A genius is someone who believes in and
takes action on the ideas that God sends him.

Tommy Newberry

Day 88

Genius is one percent inspiration
and ninety-nine percent perspiration.

Thomas Edison

There is only one success –
to be able to spend your life in your own way.

Christopher Morley

Day 89

A person who is willing to make a personal commitment to perpetual re-education with or without company support has the most exceptional opportunities known in this or any other recent century. The emphasis is on lifetime learning.

Tom Peters

Day 90

Some men have thousands of reasons why they cannot do what they want to, when all they need is one reason why they can.

Willis R. Whitney

Only the insecure strive for security.

Wayne Dyer

Day 91

In all planning,
you make a list and set your priorities.

Alan Lakein

Fatigue does make cowards of us all.

Vince Lombardi

Day 92

The place to improve the world is first in
one's own heart and head and hands.

Robert Pirsig

Do what you love.
Know your own bone;
gnaw at it, bury it,
unearth it,
and gnaw it still.

Henry David Thoreau

Realize that everything you watch, read, or listen to is influencing your behavior for good or for bad.

Tommy Newberry

DAY 93

Our duty is to proceed as if limits to our ability did not exist.

Teilhard de Chardin

Love is the river of life in this world.

Henry Ward Beecher

The first and best victory is to conquer self.

Plato

DAY 94

Day 95

Refuse to let an old person move into your body.

Wayne Dyer

You become positive by deciding in advance that you will always choose the most resourceful response to any given set of circumstances.

Tommy Newberry

Day 96

Here's my one-word formula for happiness. Growth – mental, spiritual, financial, …you name it.

Tommy Newberry

The unexamined life is not worth living.

Socrates

Day 97

Can you think of anything
more permanently elating
than to know that
you are on the right road at last?

Vernon Howard

The unplanned life is not worth examining.

Aristotle

Day 98

Worry affects circulation, the heart and the glands, the whole nervous system and profoundly affects the heart.
I have never known a man who died from over work, but many who died from doubt.

Charles H. Mayo

Day 99

The quality of a person's life is
in direct proportion
to their commitment to excellence, regardless
of their chosen field of endeavor.

Vince Lombardi

You must believe in your success to the point
that you prepare for it even when there is
no outward evidence to suggest it is plausible.

Tommy Newberry

Day 100

Circumstances! I make circumstances!

Napoleon Bonaparte

The reasonable man adapts himself to the world;
the unreasonable one persists in trying to adapt
the world to himself.
Therefore all progress depends
on the unreasonable man.

George Bernard Shaw

Day 101

I don't look at an obstacle as something that somebody's doing against me. I look at it as an opportunity to gain some character, to learn a great lesson of life, so I can turn back one day and tell somebody, "You know what? I made it through that – you can do the same thing."

Burgess Owens

Day 102

You cannot help the poor man by destroying the rich.

Abraham Lincoln

The philosophy of the rich versus the poor is this: The rich invest their money and spend what's left; the poor spend their money and invest what's left.

Jim Rohn

Self-discipline means doing within
while you do without.

Denis Waitley

Day 103

If you have tried to do something and failed,
you are vastly better off than if you had tried to
do nothing and succeeded.

If you only care enough for a result,
you will almost certainly attain it.
Only you must then really wish these things,
and wish them exclusively,
and not wish at the same time
a hundred other incompatible things
just as strongly.

William James

Day 104

Others can stop you temporarily;
only you can do it permanently.

Day 105

Let him learn a prudence of a higher strain.
Let him learn that everything in nature,
even dust and feathers, go by law and not by luck.
And that what he sows, he reaps.

Ralph Waldo Emerson

What is now proved was only once imagined.

William Blake

Day 106

Few men during their lifetime
come anywhere near exhausting
the resources dwelling within them.
There are deep wells of strength
that are never used.

Richard Byrd

Day 107

The Lord works from the inside out.
The world works from the outside in.
The world would take people out of the slums.
Christ takes the slums out of people,
and then they take themselves out of the slums.
The world would mold men
by changing their environment.
Christ changes men,
who then change their environment.
The world would shape human behavior,
but Christ can change human nature.

Ezra Taft Benson

The sky is not less blue because
the blind man does not see it.

Danish Proverb

Day 108

The quotations when engraved upon the
memory give you good thoughts.
They also make you anxious to read the authors
and look for more.

Winston Churchill

Life is really simple,
but men insist on making it complicated.

Confucius

DAY 109

Sow a thought, reap an action;
Sow an action, reap a habit;
Sow a habit, reap a character;
Sow a character, reap a destiny.

Every experience in life, everything with which we have come in contact in life is a chisel which has been cutting away at our life statue, molding, modifying, shaping it. We are part of all we have met. Everything we have seen, heard, felt, or thought has had its hand in molding and shaping us.

Orison Swett Marden

DAY 110

> Confidence in yourself
> shows confidence in your Creator.
>
> *Tommy Newberry*

Day 111

> Great minds discuss ideas,
> average minds discuss events,
> small minds discuss people.
>
> *Hyman G. Rickover*

> Most behavior is controlled by habits.
> When you choose a habit,
> you also choose the results
> that go with that habit.
> Create positive habits
> that help you produce.
>
> *Merrill Douglass*

Day 112

Nothing speaks louder than results.
Happiness is a dividend on a well-invested life.

Duncan Stuart

What's your excuse?

Slogan of the Paralympic Games

Day 113

A wise man will make more opportunities than he finds.

Francis Bacon

What you think of me is none of my business.

Terry Cole Whittaker

Day 114

Day 115

The first step you take to creating the results
you want is to assertively take strategic
control of your environment – of what
you are exposed to on a consistent basis.

Tommy Newberry

Great men are they who see the spiritual is
stronger than material force,
that thoughts rule the world.

Ralph Waldo Emerson

Day 116

The one thing over which you have
absolute control is your own thoughts.
It is this that puts you in a position
to control your own destiny.

Paul G. Thomas

Day 117

Are you in earnest?
Seek this very minute,
whatever you can do,
or dream you can; begin it.
Boldness has genius, power and magic in it.
Only engage and the mind grows heated;
begin and then the task will be completed.

Goethe

Day 118

As long as you know what it is you desire,
then by simply affirming that it is yours –
firmly and positively, with no ifs, buts, or
maybes – over and over again, from the minute
you arise in the morning until the time you go to
sleep at night, and as many times during the day
as your work or activities permit,
you will be drawn to those people, places,
and events that will bring your desires to you.

Scott Reed

Day 119

For better it is to dare mighty things,
to win glorious triumphs,
even though checkered by failure,
than to rank with those poor spirits
who neither enjoy much nor suffer much,
because they live in the twilight
that knows not victory nor defeat.

Theodore Roosevelt

Day 120

Man is a goal seeking animal.
His life only has meaning if he is
reaching out and striving for his goals.

Aristotle

Where there is no vision, the people perish.

Proverbs 29:18

Day 121

Perhaps nobody ever accomplishes all that he feels lies in him to do; but nearly everyone who tries his powers touches the walls of his being.

Charles Dudley Warner

Show me a thoroughly satisfied man, and I will show you a failure.

Thomas Edison

Day 122

Our rewards in life will always be in direct proportion to our contribution.

Earl Nightingale

You must be single-minded. Drive for the one thing on which you have decided.

George Patton

Day 123

Make no little plans;
they have no magic to stir
men's blood and probably
themselves will not be realized.
Make big plans;
aim high in hope and work,
remembering that a noble,
logical diagram once recorded will not die.

Daniel H. Burnham

Day 124

It is our calling that makes us think beyond the
demands and pettiness of today and causes us to
focus on all that we can be and can do for God
and for good in all of our todays and
all of our tomorrows.

W. Frank Harrington

N o one's happiness but my own
is in my power to achieve or to destroy.

Ayn Rand

DAY 125

An extraordinary life is simply the accumulation
of thousands of efforts, often unseen by others,
that lead to the accomplishment
of worthwhile goals.

Tommy Newberry

Growth means change and
change involves risks,
stepping from the known
to the unknown.

George Shinn

DAY 126

A successful person is one
who can lay a firm foundation
with the bricks that others throw at him.

Day 127

Develop the habit of always doing
what you say you'll do.
This strengthens your character
and programs yourself to create
the reality dictated by your words.

Tommy Newberry

Day 128

Every street is paved with gold.

Kim Woo - Choong

Adversity is the first path to Truth.

Lord Byron

Day 129

Friendship
is a strong and habitual inclination
in two persons
to promote the good and happiness
of one another.

Eustace Budgell

Day 130

Man must cease attributing his problems
to his environment,
and learn again to exercise his will...
his personal responsibility.

Albert Schweitzer

Day 131

No one can cheat you out of ultimate success but yourself.

Ralph Waldo Emerson

Day 132

Surround yourself with positive, success driven people – individuals who want to achieve big things and contribute to the world in tremendous ways.

Tommy Newberry

Iron sharpens iron and one man sharpens another.

Proverbs 22:17

Opportunity is the best captain
of all endeavor.

Sophocles

There's no hopeless situation until you become a hopeless person.

Robert Schuller

DAY 133

The people who get on in this world are
the people who get up and look
for the circumstances they want,
and, if they can't find them, make them.

George Bernard Shaw

DAY 134

Day 135

Responsible persons are mature people
who have taken charge of themselves
and their conduct,
who own their actions and own up to them –
who answer for them.

William Bennett

Day 136

You can never hear the truth too many times.

Tommy Newberry

He that won't be counseled can't be helped.

Benjamin Franklin

Most players are pretty good, but they go to
where the puck is.
I go to where the puck is going to be.

Wayne Gretzky

DAY 137

I do not want anybody to convince my son
that someone will guarantee him a living.
I want him rather to realize that there is plenty
of opportunity in this country for him to achieve
success but whether he wins or loses depends
entirely on his own character, perseverance,
thrift, intelligence and capacity for hard work.

John L. Griffith

DAY 138

Day 139

Keep away from people who try
to belittle your ambitions.
Small people always do that,
but the really great make you feel that you,
too, can become great.

Mark Twain

What is the most magnificent goal
you can pursue in the next three years?

Tommy Newberry

Day 140

Man, alone, has the power
to transform his thoughts
into physical reality;
man, alone, can dream
and make his dreams come true.

Napoleon Hill

DAY 141

All who have accomplished great things
have had a great aim,
have fixed their gaze on a goal which was high,
one which sometimes seemed impossible.

Orison Swett Marden

DAY 142

The happiness of your life
depends upon the quality of your thoughts,
therefore, guard accordingly.

Marcus Antonius

If you can believe,
all things are possible
to him who believes.

Mark 9:23

DAY 143

See, anyone can be a high achiever.
The difference with high achievers,
with peak performers,
is that they have simply
developed more of their
God-given potential.

Tommy Newberry

A great pleasure in life is doing
what people say you cannot do.

Walter Gagehot

DAY 144

Nature is at work.
Character and destiny are her handiwork.
She gives us love and hate,
jealousy and reverence.
All that is ours is the power to choose
which impulse we shall follow.

David Seabury

Let us train our minds to desire what the
situation demands.

Lucius Annaeus Seneca

Day 145

Your outlook upon life, your estimate
of yourself, your estimate of your value are
largely colored by your environment…
Your whole career will be modified, shaped,
molded by your surroundings,
by the character of the people with whom you
come in contact everyday…

Orison Swett Marden

Day 146

The only certain means of success is to render
more and better service than is expected of you,
no matter what your task may be.

Og Mandino

Those who say winning isn't everything
have probably never won anything.

Day 147

I bargained with Life for a penny,
And Life would pay no more,
However I begged at evening
When I counted my scanty store.
For Life is a just employer,
He gives you what you ask,
But once you have set the wages,
Why, you must bear the task.
I worked for a menial's hire,
Only to learn, dismayed,
That any wage I had asked of Life,
Life would have willingly paid.

Day 148

Fear is the most powerful of all thoughts
with one exception, and that
one exception is faith.

Norman Vincent Peale

What you think and talk about
   expands into action.

Wayne Dyer

DAY 149

Far away there in the sunshine
   are my highest aspirations.
   I may not reach them,
but I can look up and see their beauty,
   believe in them, and try to follow
      where they lead.

Louisa May Alcott

If we all did the things we are capable of doing,
   we could literally astound ourselves.

Thomas Edison

DAY 150

"I don't think I can" rises from the deeper,
   "I don't think I am."

Robert Schuller

Day 151

> You will know them by their fruits.
>
> *Matthew 7:16*

> Correct your attitudes and actions and leave the results to God.
>
> *Larry Burkette*

Day 152

> The reward of a thing well done is to have done it.
>
> *Ralph Waldo Emerson*

> And whoever compels you to go one mile, go with him two.
>
> *Matthew 5:41*

DAY 153

Goals provide you with clarity of outcome which is the prerequisite for becoming an outstanding decision maker.

Tommy Newberry

The great dividing line between success and failure can be expressed in five words: I did not have time.

DAY 154

The greatest power that a person possesses is the power to choose.

J. Martin Kohe

No man need live a minute longer as he is because the Creator endowed him with the ability to change himself.

J.C. Penney

What the caterpillar calls the end of the world,
the Master calls the butterfly.

Richard Bach

Day 155

As in water, face answers to face,
so the mind of man reflects the man.

Proverbs 27:19

You cannot strengthen the weak
by weakening the strong.

Abraham Lincoln

Day 156

I've learned one important thing. I can do anything I think I can –
but I can't do anything alone. No one can go it alone. Create your team!

Robert Schuller

Day 157

Happy are those who dream dreams
and are ready to pay the price
to make them come true.

Leon J. Suenens

Man is not the creature of circumstances;
circumstances are the creature of man.

Benjamin Disraeli

Day 158

He that wrestles with us strengthens
our nerves and sharpens our skill.
Our antagonist is our helper.

Edmund Burke

Hidden talent counts for nothing.

Nero

Day 159

Misbelieving turns into misbehaving.
Right thoughts never produce wrong actions.
Remember, a good tree won't bear bad fruit.

Tommy Newberry

Day 160

Problems are to the mind
what exercise is to the muscles,
they toughen and make strong.

Norman Vincent Peale

Success is the systematic, progressive and deliberate accomplishment of God's will in your life. It just doesn't happen accidentally.

Tommy Newberry

DAY 161

Success is a state of mind.
If you want success,
start thinking of yourself
as a success.

Joyce Brothers

DAY 162

Day 163

If a person must wait until something happens to make him happy, he's not going to get much fun out of life.

Earl Nightingale

We are all faced with magnificent opportunities, brilliantly disguised as impossible situations.

Charles R. Swindoll

Day 164

The law of gravity is evident when you drop something. The law of belief is evident when you do something. Watch what you do and you'll know what you believe.

Tommy Newberry

Day 165

Until one is committed, there is hesitancy, the chance to draw back, always ineffectiveness. Concerning all acts of initiative (and creation), there is an elementary truth, the ignorance of which kills countless ideas and splendid plans; that the moment one definitely commits oneself, then Providence moves, too.

All sorts of things occur to help that would never otherwise have occurred. A whole stream of events issues from the decision, raising in one's favor all manner of unforeseen incidents and meetings and material assistance, which no man could have dreamed would have come his way.

Charles Murray

Day 166

The easiest thing to do in the world is to neglect the important and give in to the urgent.

Denis Waitley

Day 167

We are what we repeatedly do.
Excellence, then, is not an act, but a habit.

Aristotle

Clarity Attracts!
Clarity precedes productivity.

Tommy Newberry

Day 168

Don't wish it were easier; wish you were better.
Don't wish for less problems; wish for more skills.
Don't wish for less challenges;
wish for more wisdom.

Jim Rohn

Strength and growth come only through
continuous effort and struggle.

Napoleon Hill

You are where you are today because you've chosen to be there.

Harry Browne

DAY 169

Well begun is half done.

Aristotle

Know thyself.

Socrates

Love does not consist in gazing at each other,
but in looking outward,
together in the same direction.

Antoine de Saint-Exupéry

DAY 170

Day 171

What do I mean by concentration?
I mean focusing totally on the business at hand
and commanding your body to do
exactly what you want it to do.

Arnold Palmer

Day 172

The choice is yours. You hold the tiller.
You can steer the course you choose
in the direction of where you want to be –
today, tomorrow, or in the distant time to come.

W. Clement Stone

Patience is a necessary ingredient of genius.

Benjamin Disraeli

The price of success is perseverance.
The price of failure comes cheaper.

DAY 173

The desire not to be anything is
the desire not to be.

Ayn Rand

Life will always be to a large extent what we
ourselves make it.

Samuel Smiles

DAY 174

Day 175

Feed your mind with thoughts
that cause it to be peaceful.
To have a mind full of peace
merely fill it full of peace.
It's as simple as that.

Norman Vincent Peale

Day 176

I have learned that success is to be measured
not so much by the position
that one has reached in life
as by the obstacles
which he has overcome
while trying to succeed.

Booker T. Washington

Never settle for less
than you can be
in any area of your life.

Tommy Newberry

Day 177

A workout is a wise use of time
and an investment in excellence.
It is a way of preparing for life's challenges
and proving to yourself
that you have what it takes
to do what is necessary.

George Allen

Day 178

Hold yourself responsible for a higher standard
than anybody else expects of you.
Never excuse yourself.

Henry Ward Beecher

Day 179

To create a highly paid job,
you must become highly productive.
No one else can do it for you.

Brian Tracy

You must choose the thoughts and actions that
will lead you on to success.

R. C. Allen

Day 180

The secret of success lies not
in doing your own work,
but in recognizing the right man to do it.

Andrew Carnegie

We are shaped and fashioned by what we love.

Goethe

The best thing about the future is that it comes only one day at a time.

Abraham Lincoln

DAY 181

Success seems to be largely a matter of hanging on after others have let go.

William Feather

Character is destiny.

Heraclitus

DAY 182

Day 183

Succeeding in America is easy!
That's why everyone wants to come here.
People haven't plotted and schemed for the last fifty years saying,
"If I could just get to Poland everything would be okay."

Jim Rohn

Day 184

The spirit of self-help is the root of all genuine growth in the individual;
and, exhibited in the lives of many,
it constitutes the true source
of national vigor and strength.
Help from without is often enfeebling in its effects, but help from within
invariably invigorates.

Samuel Smiles

As you become more prosperous
in your thinking you become like a color blind
child in a fabulous garden
suddenly able to see the rich images
that have been there all along.

Tommy Newberry

Day 185

Success consists of a series
of little daily victories.

Laddie F. Hutar

If a man only does what is required of him,
he is a slave –
the moment he begins to do more
than he is required,
he becomes a free man.

Day 186

Day 187

Give me a stock clerk with a goal and I will give you a man who will make history.
Give me a man without a goal and I will give you a stock clerk.

J.C. Penney

Day 188

Since greatness is possible, then being excellent is not enough.

Les Brown

He who has a why to live can bear almost any how.

Friedrich Wilhelm Nietzsche

Whatever you're ready for
is ready for you.

Mark Victor Hansen

You will become as small
as your controlling desire;
or as great as your dominant aspiration.

James Allen

DAY 189

Success in life comes from one thing,
from deciding exactly what it is
you want to accomplish
and then deliberately choosing to invest
the minutes and hours of your life doing only
those things that move you in the direction
of your goals.

Tommy Newberry

DAY 190

One person with belief is equal
to a force of 99 who only have interest.

John Stuart Mill

Day 191

Realizing that our actions, feelings,
and behavior are the result of our own images
and beliefs gives us the lever that psychology has
always needed for changing personality.

Maxwell Maltz

A man's life is what his thoughts make of it.

Marcus Aurelius

Day 192

The greatest test of courage on earth is to bear
defeat without losing heart.

Robert Ingersoll

Day 193

Most people live, whether physically, intellectually or morally, in a very restricted circle of their potential being. They make use of a very small portion of their possible consciousness, and of their soul's resources in general, much like a man who, out of his whole bodily organism, should get into a habit of using and moving only his little finger. Great emergencies and crises show us how much greater our vital resources are than we had supposed.

William James

Day 194

Trying to do something big and failing is infinitely better than trying to do very little and succeeding.

Tommy Newberry

To everything there is a season, a time for every purpose under the heaven.

Ecclesiastes 3:1

The future of this republic
is in the hands of the American voter.

Dwight Eisenhower

Day 195

Properly, we should read for power.
Man reading should be man intensely alive.
The book should be a ball of light in one's hand.

Ezra Pound

Day 196

A man sooner or later discovers that he
is the master-gardener
of his soul, the director of his life.

James Allen

Day 197

Y̲ou will succeed to the degree
that you are willing
to accelerate your rate of failure.

Tommy Newberry

Day 198

E̲ntrepreneur:
He casts aside his assurance of 40-hour weeks,
leaves the safe cover of tenure and security,
and charges across the perilous fields of change
and opportunity.
If he succeeds, his profits will come not from
what he takes from his fellow citizens,
but from the value they freely place on the gift of
his imagination.

George Gilder

Tell him to live by yes and no –
yes to everything good, no to everything bad.

William James

Day 199

There are four steps to accomplishment:

> Plan Purposefully
> Prepare Prayerfully
> Proceed Positively
> Pursue Persistently

To be innocent is to be not guilty;
but to be virtuous is to overcome
our evil inclinations.

William Penn

Day 200

Desire is proof of the availability...

Robert Collier

Constant improvement is no longer a luxury but a necessity. The only option you have is to increase your value every single day.

Tommy Newberry

DAY 201

The empires of the future are the empires of the mind.

Winston Churchill

There is an infinite difference between a little wrong and just right, between fairly good and the best, between mediocrity and superiority.

Orison Swett Marden

DAY 202

Day 203

Courage is the capacity to confront what can be imagined.

Leo Rosten

If not you, then who?
If not now, then when?

Hillel

Day 204

Truth is the property of no individual but is the treasure of all men.

Ralph Waldo Emerson

DAY 205

You can walk up to the ocean of abundance
with either a thimble or a tanker truck.
Most, unfortunately, choose the thimble
never even knowing that there was an alternative.

Tommy Newberry

DAY 206

Life in abundance
comes only through great love.

Elbert Hubbard

Behavior is the perpetual revealing of us.
What a man does, tells us what he is.

F.D. Huntington

Day 207

I'm a great believer in luck, and I find the harder I work the more I have of it.

Thomas Jefferson

All things are difficult before they are easy.

Thomas Fuller

Day 208

A merry heart does good, like medicine.

Proverbs 17:22

High achievers avoid reaching into too many baskets.

Tommy Newberry

Neutrality is a decision. It is a decision to do nothing. Games are not won by those who sit on the bench, but by those who get in the game!

W. Frank Harrington

Day 209

You can get everything in life you want if you help enough other people get what they want.

Zig Ziglar

Excellence is the gradual result of always wanting to do better.

Pat Riley

Day 210

DAY 211

One of the most beautiful compensations of life is that no man can sincerely try to help another without helping himself.

Ralph Waldo Emerson

People show what they are by what they do with what they have.

DAY 212

The only way to find the limits of the possible is by going beyond them to the impossible.

Arthur C. Clarke

If a man empties his purse into his head,
no man can take it away from him.
An investment in knowledge always
pays the best dividends.

Benjamin Franklin

DAY 213

Whatever you direct your mind to think
about will ultimately be revealed
for everyone to see.

Tommy Newberry

DAY 214

Day 215

Do the thing and you will have the power.

Ralph Waldo Emerson

Nothing happens unless first a dream.

Carl Sandburg

Day 216

He that walketh with wise men shall be wise.

Proverbs 13:20

I do not fear failure. I only fear the "slowing up" of the engine inside of me which is pounding, saying, "keep going, someone must be on top, why not you?"

George Patton

Day 217

The only thing that stands between a man
and what he wants from life is often merely
the will to try it and the faith to believe that it
is possible.

Richard M. DeVos

You can't steal second
and keep your foot on first.

Day 218

The mind is its own place,
and in itself can make a heaven of hell,
a hell of heaven.

John Milton

A successful person is one who accomplishes
goals and is able to enjoy the fruits of them.

Larry Burkette

Day 219

There is no such thing as playing
over your head.
What appears to be such is simply
a view of your true potential.

Bob Rotella

A foolish consistency is
the hobgoblin of small minds.

Ralph Waldo Emerson

Day 220

Before a gold mine comes a goal mind!

Tommy Newberry

The only thing about a man that is a man
is his mind.
Everything else you can find
in a pig or a horse.

Archibald MacLeish

Day 221

What happens is not as important as
how you react to what happens.

Thaddeus Golas

Give, and it will be given to you:
good measure, pressed down, shaken together,
and running over…

Luke 6:38

Day 222

Do all the good you can,
By all the means you can,
In all the ways you can,
In all the places you can,
At all the times you can,
To all the people you can,
As long as ever you can.

John Wesley

Day 223

Mother must have been a pretty special motivator, because I took her seriously when she told me I should always try to be the best I could at whatever I took on.
So, I have always pursued everything I was interested in with true passion –
some would say obsession – to win. I've always held the bar pretty high for myself:
I've set extremely high personal goals.

Sam Walton

Day 224

The more specific and measurable your goal, the more quickly you will be able to identify, locate, create and implement the use of the necessary resources for its achievement.

Tommy Newberry

You cannot build character and courage by taking away a man's initiative and independence.

Abraham Lincoln

DAY 225

A lazy person affects the one he works for like vinegar on the teeth or smoke in the eyes.

Proverbs 10:26

Much that passes off for education is nothing more than a social agenda, bereft of even common sense, masquerading as progress. The hollow lives that fill countless news stories or live in anguished silence reveal the price paid for the belief that truth as a category does not exist.

Ravi Zacharias

DAY 226

A person cannot travel within
and stand still without.

James Allen

Day 227

A good man out of the good treasure
of his heart brings forth good;
and an evil man out the evil treasure
of his heart brings forth evil.
For out of the abundance
of the heart his mouth speaks.

Luke 6:45

All growth depends upon activity.
There is no development...
without effort...
Work is... the only means to manhood.

Calvin Coolidge

Day 228

Sow much, reap much;
Sow little, reap little.

Chinese Proverb

Day 229

Do what you love
and you'll stop being
your own worst enemy.

Tommy Newberry

It is the mind that maketh good or ill,
that maketh wretch or happy, rich or poor.

Edmund Spenser

Day 230

There is no security on this earth.
There is only opportunity.

Douglas MacArthur

The human mind,
once stretched by a new idea,
never regains its original dimensions.

Oliver Wendell Holmes

If you don't run your own life,
somebody else will.

John Atkinson

DAY 231

Nature cannot be tricked or cheated.
She will give up to you the object
of your struggles
only after you have paid her price.

Napoleon Hill

Two things make a champion.
Pride and work.
I don't know that I've ever
been around a champion,
a true champion year in and year out,
unless he was working,
always trying to get better.

Jimmy Johnson

DAY 232

DAY 233

Always bear in mind
that your own resolution
to succeed
is more important
than any other one thing.

Abraham Lincoln

Add up your joys and
never count your sorrows.

Robert Schuller

DAY 234

Winning is not a sometime thing;
it's an all time thing.
You don't win once in a while,
you don't do things right once in a while,
you do them right all the time.
Winning is a habit.
Unfortunately, so is losing.

Vince Lombardi

Day 235

There is nothing capricious in nature
and the implanting of a desire
indicates that its gratification is
in the constitution
of the creature that feels it.

Ralph Waldo Emerson

Success starts on the inside and
spreads to the outside.

Tommy Newberry

Day 236

I recommend you to take care of the minutes,
for the hours will take care of themselves.

Lord Chesterfield

Two men look out through the same bars:
one sees the mud, and one the stars.

Frederick Langbridge

DAY 237

You were created and blessed
with unlimited potential,
with the ability to make your life a masterpiece.

Tommy Newberry

Luck is not chance – It's toil –
Fortune's expensive smile is earned.

Emily Dickinson

DAY 238

When an archer misses the mark,
he turns and looks for the fault within himself.
Failure to hit the bull's eye
is never the fault of the target.
To improve your aim – improve yourself.

Gilbert Arland

I know of no more encouraging fact than the
unquestionable ability of man to elevate his life
by conscious endeavor.

Henry David Thoreau

There are no contradictions.

Ayn Rand

Day 239

You are responsible for the thoughts
you have in your head at any given time.
You have the capacity to think whatever you
choose, and virtually all your self-defeating
attitudes and behaviors
originate in the way you choose to think.

Wayne Dyer

Good is not good
When better is expected.

Thomas Fuller

Day 240

Neglect is a silent killer.

Tommy Newberry

You cannot help men permanently
by doing for them
what they could and should do.....themselves.

Abraham Lincoln

Only in growth, reform, and change,
paradoxically enough, is true security
to be found.

Anne Morrow Lindberg

DAY 241

The greatest discovery of my generation
is that human beings can alter their lives
by altering their attitudes of mind.

William James

I've never been poor, only broke.
Being poor is a frame of mind.
Being broke is only a temporary situation.

Mike Todd

DAY 242

> The moment you give up all thought
> of surrender or retreat you become
> an unstoppable force.
>
> *Tommy Newberry*

DAY 243

> It isn't the people you fire
> who make your life miserable,
> it's the people you don't.
>
> *Harvey Mackay*

> What lies behind us
> and what lies before us
> are tiny matters
> compared to what lies within us.
>
> *Ralph Waldo Emerson*

DAY 244

> Goal setting is the strongest human force
> for self-motivation.
>
> *Paul J. Meyer*

You may be whatever you resolve to be.

Stonewall Jackson

You have to sow before you can reap.
You have to give before you can get.

Robert Collier

DAY 245

One man has enthusiasm for 30 minutes,
another for 30 days,
but it is the man who has it for 30 years
who makes a success of his life.

Edward B. Butler

Do what you fear most and you control fear.

Tom Hopkins

DAY 246

All great achievements take time.

David Schwartz

Day 247

For children to take morality seriously
they must be in the presence of adults
who take morality seriously.
And with their own eyes they must see
adults take morality seriously.

William Bennett

We are all born for love.
It is the principle of existence,
and its only end.

Benjamin Disraeli

Day 248

What are you willing to do differently
to become the person you want
to become?

Tommy Newberry

DAY 249

Once a belief is locked in, you tend to notice only those things which reinforce or create additional evidence that your belief is true.

Tommy Newberry

Don't pray for dreams equal to your powers. Pray for powers equal to your dreams.

DAY 250

The successful man will profit
from his mistakes and
try again in a different way.

Dale Carnegie

Those who pursue the higher life of wisdom, who seek to live by spiritual principles, must be prepared to be laughed at and condemned.

Epictetus

Prefer a loss to a dishonest gain;
the one brings pain at the moment,
the other for all time.

Chilon

Day 251

I believe that you can get
everything in life you want
if you will just help enough other people
to get what they want.

Zig Ziglar

Be still and know that I am God.

Psalm 46:10

I never did a day's work in my life.
It was all fun.

Thomas Edison

Day 252

366 Days of Wisdom & Inspiration

You should be very interested in your future...
because you are destined to spend
the rest of your life there.

Tommy Newberry

And if a house be divided against itself,
that house cannot stand.

Mark 3:25

Day 253

Nothing is impossible to a willing heart.

John Heywood

If a man does not keep pace
with his companions,
perhaps it is because he hears
a different drummer.
Let him step to the music which he hears,
however measured or far away.

Henry David Thoreau

Day 254

Day 255

Don't be afraid to fail.
Don't waste energy trying to cover up failure.
Learn from your failures and go on
to the next challenge.
It's OK.
If you're not failing,
you're not growing.

H. Stanley Judd

Day 256

Nature imitates itself.
A grain thrown into good ground
brings forth fruit;
a principle thrown into a good mind
brings forth fruit.
Everything is created and conducted
by the same Master:
the root, the branch, the fruits –
the principles, the consequences.

Blaise Pascal

Let him that would move the world,
first move himself.

Socrates

High achievers are motivated
by pleasurable outcomes.
Under achievers are motivated
by pleasurable methods.

Tommy Newberry

DAY 257

Today's self talk is tomorrow's reality.

Tommy Newberry

Would you let a murderer into your house?
Of course not.
Then why let ideas that murder your goals
into your head?

Joey Reiman

DAY 258

Nothing has any power over me
other than that which I give it
through my conscious thoughts.

Tony Robbins

DAY 259

You can start right where you stand and
apply the habit of going the extra mile
by rendering more service and better service
than you are now being paid for.

Napoleon Hill

Being in power is like being a lady.
If you have to tell people you are, you aren't.

Margaret Thatcher

DAY 260

DAY 261

In reading the lives of great men,
I found that the first victory they won was
over themselves...self-discipline with
all of them came first.

Harry Truman

Failure is only the opportunity
to more intelligently begin again.

Henry Ford

DAY 262

A man, as a general rule, owes very little
to what he is born with –
a man is what he makes of himself.

Alexander Graham Bell

Demand more from yourself
than others expect.

Tommy Newberry

Day 263

We begin to see, therefore, the importance of selecting our environment with the greatest of care because environment is the mental feeding ground out of which the food that goes into our minds is extracted.

Napoleon Hill

Day 264

Personal development allows for the unfolding of your unique talents and gifts. It is the gradual improvement and perfection of your character. It is the mature realization that no one is coming to the rescue, that your circumstances are but a reflection of your inner self, and that if your life is to change, you must change.

Tommy Newberry

Day 265

Never tell people how to do things.
Tell them what to do and they will
surprise you with their ingenuity.

George Patton

The secret of success
is the consistency to pursue.

Harry Banks

Day 266

The world makes way for the man who knows
where he is going.

Ralph Waldo Emerson

Don't worry about the past.
Yesterday is as out of reach
as one thousand years ago.
Tomorrow, though, can and will be shaped
by today's choices.

Tommy Newberry

Day 267

If you want to succeed you should strike out on new paths rather than travel the worn paths of accepted success.

John D. Rockefeller, Jr.

You have to think big to be big.

Claude Bristol

Day 268

In my mind, talent plus knowledge, plus effort account for success.

Gertrude Samuels

Successful people are not people without problems; they're simply people who've learned to solve their problems.

Robert Seashore

Visible circumstances are the effect
of invisible thought.

Tommy Newberry

Destiny is not a matter of chance;
it is a matter of choice.
It is not something to be waited for;
but rather something to be achieved.

William Jennings Bryan

DAY 269

A workout is a personal triumph over laziness
and procrastination.
It is the badge of a winner, the mark of an
organized, goal oriented person
who has taken charge of his or her own destiny.

George Allen

DAY 270

There are no victories at bargain prices.

Dwight D. Eisenhower

DAY 271

You can't afford the luxury
of a negative thought.

John Roger and Peter McWilliams

I hear and I forget.
I see and I remember.
I do and I understand.

Chinese Proverb

DAY 272

Some people change jobs,
mates and friends,
but never think of changing themselves.

366 Days of Wisdom & Inspiration

Success comes to those
who become success conscious.
Failure comes to those
who indifferently allow themselves
to become failure conscious.

Napoleon Hill

The will to succeed is important,
but what's more important
is the will to prepare.

Bobby Knight

Day 273

The very act of writing down and
setting magnificent and compelling goals
unlocks your creative powers
and the act of writing down your goals in detail
is completely under your control.

Tommy Newberry

Day 274

The quality of a leader is reflected in
the standards he sets for himself.

Ray Kroc

Day 275

Our doubts are traitors,
and make us lose the good we oft might win,
by fearing to attempt.

William Shakespeare

Greatness lies not in being strong,
but in the right use of strength.

Henry Ward Beecher

As you believe, so you behave.

Tommy Newberry

Day 276

Practice a daily quiet time in which to listen
intently for God's direction,
listen more deeply than your own thoughts.

Norman Vincent Peale

DAY 277

Go as far as you can see,
and when you get there,
you will see farther still.

Hold to your true aspirations
no matter what is going on around you.

Epictetus

DAY 278

If you clutter your mind with little things,
will there be any room left for big things?

Common sense in an uncommon degree
is what the world calls wisdom.

Samuel Coleridge

DAY 279

The problem with most leaders today
is they don't stand for anything.
Leadership implies movement toward something,
and convictions provide that direction.
If you don't stand for something,
you'll fall for anything.

Don Shula

You can never outgrow your self-concept;
you can only replace it.

Tommy Newberry

DAY 280

To change one's life:
Start immediately,
do it flamboyantly,
no exceptions.

William James

Habit is either the best of servants
or the worst of masters.

Nathaniel Emmons

If you think you can, you can;
If you think you can't, you can't.

Henry Ford

DAY 281

One of the most powerful influences
on your character, personality, and attitude
is what you say to yourself and believe.

Tommy Newberry

It is always your next move.

Napoleon Hill

DAY 282

The past does not equal the future.

Tony Robbins

DAY 283

You'll always miss 100%
of the shots you don't take.

Never think or talk lack for in so doing you are
decreeing lack. Stress the thought of plenty.
Thoughts of plenty help create plenty.

Norman Vincent Peale

DAY 284

Anything less than a conscious commitment
to the important
is an unconscious commitment to unimportant.

Stephen Covey

We must cultivate our garden.

Voltaire

DAY 285

Do you want your Big But
or do you want your goal?
You can't have both.

Tommy Newberry

The individual who goes the farthest is generally
the one who is willing to do, dare
and attempt new things.
The sure thing boat never gets far from shore.

Dale Carnegie

DAY 286

No one could make a greater mistake
than he who did nothing
because he could do only a little.

Edmund Burke

The ladder of success
does not care who climbs it.

Frank Tyger

Day 287

First you take action,
then you'll get motivated.
Not the other way around.

Joey Reiman

The words we use create the world we see.

Tommy Newberry

Day 288

No man is ever whipped,
until he quits –
in his own mind.

Napoleon Hill

The thing always happens
that you really believe in;
and the belief in a thing
makes it happen.

Frank Lloyd Wright

DAY 289

Change the changeable, accept the unchangeable,
and remove yourself from the unacceptable.

Denis Waitley

You don't pay the price for success.
You enjoy the price for success.

Zig Ziglar

DAY 290

Day 291

Vacillating people seldom succeed.
They seldom win the solid respect
of their fellows.
Successful men and women are very careful
in reaching decisions and very persistent
and determined in action thereafter.

L.G. Elliott

A problem is a chance for you to do your best.

Duke Ellington

Day 292

Can success change the human mechanism
so completely between one dawn and another?
Can it make one feel taller, more alive,
handsomer, uncommonly gifted and indomitably
secure with the certainty that this is the way life
will always be? It can and it does!

Moss Hart

Day 293

Be wiser than other people,
if you can,
but do not tell them so.

Lord Chesterfield

Successful men and women train their minds
to only think about what they want
to have happen in their lives.

Tommy Newberry

Day 294

It is only because of problems
that we grow mentally and spiritually.

M. Scott Peck

A lazy person will end up poor,
but a hard worker will become rich.

Proverbs 10:4

All things be ready if our minds be so.

William Shakespeare

Day 295

Mindsight is the power to see not what is
but what can be when
human intelligence is applied.
Mindsight is the power to dream…
Mindsight is purely spiritual and
sees only potentiality.

David Schwartz

How sweet it is to stand
on the edge of tomorrow.

Robert Schuller

Day 296

Your talent, skill, and creativity will rise to meet
the level of goal you set for yourself.
So think HUGE!

Tommy Newberry

Day 297

The successful person always has a number of projects planned, to which he looks forward. Any one of them could change the course of his life overnight.

Mark Caine

Life is like playing a violin in public and learning the instrument as one goes on.

Samuel Butler

Day 298

The majority of men meet with failure because of their lack of persistence in creating new plans to take the place of those which fail.

Napoleon Hill

But if a man happens to find himself, he has a mansion which he can inhabit with dignity all the days of his life.

James Michener

Day 299

Always try to do something for the other fellow and you will be agreeably surprised how things come your way – how many pleasant things are done for you.

Claude M. Bristol

Always forgive your enemies – nothing annoys them so much.

Oscar Wilde

Day 300

Rationalize really means rational lies.

Tommy Newberry

Death is not the greatest loss in life. The greatest loss is what dies inside us while we live.

Norman Cousins

Be not afraid, only believe.

Mark 5:36

Men grind and grind in the mill of a truism,
and nothing comes out but what was put in.
But the moment they desert the tradition for a spontaneous thought,
then poetry, wit, hope, virtue, learning, anecdote,
all flock to their aid.

Ralph Waldo Emerson

DAY 301

If you sit and relax and get yourself in tune with
God and open yourself to the flow of His power,
then sitting is not laziness, in fact,
it is about the best way to renew a person.

Norman Vincent Peale

DAY 302

Day 303

Nothing splendid has ever been achieved except by those who dared believe that something inside of them was superior to circumstance.

Bruce Barton

Things do not change; we change.

Henry David Thoreau

Day 304

The greatest asset of any nation
is the spirit of its people,
and the greatest danger
that can menace any nation
is the breakdown of that spirit –
the will to win and the courage to work.

George Courtelyou

Day 305

One of the great tragedies of modern society
is that we have herds of discontented and
underachieving people
trudging around blaming everyone
and everything for their lack of success.
These people refuse to put the responsibility for
their lives where it belongs –
with the person staring them back in the mirror.

Tommy Newberry

Day 306

Wealth is the product
of man's capacity to think.

Ayn Rand

If you are not financially independent
by the time you are forty or fifty,
it doesn't mean that you are living in the wrong
country or at the wrong time.
It simply means that you have the wrong plan.

Jim Rohn

Day 307

Since the mind is a specific biocomputer,
it needs specific instructions and directions.
The reason most people never reach their goals
is that they don't define them,
learn about them, or seriously consider
them as believable or achievable.
Winners can tell you where they are going,
what they plan to do along the way,
and who will be sharing the adventure
with them.

Denis Waitley

Day 308

Constantly think in terms of success,
in terms of victory,
and in terms of abundance.

Paul Yonggi Cho

Do not follow where the path may lead.
Go instead where there is no path and leave a
trail so that others may follow.

Day 309

Prosperity is too apt to prevent us
from examining our conduct;
but adversity leads us to think properly of our
state, and so is most beneficial to us.

Samuel Johnson

The highest honor bestowed on an individual
is the belief that he deserves the highest honor...

Tommy Boland

Day 310

What would you attempt to do if you knew you
could not fail?

Robert Schuller

The creative mechanism within you
is impersonal.
It will work automatically and impersonally
to achieve goals of success and happiness,
or unhappiness and failure,
depending on the goals which
you yourself set for it.

Maxwell Maltz

Day 311

In the confrontation between
the stream and the rock,
the stream always wins –
not through strength
but by perseverance.

H. Jackson Brown

True silence is the rest of the mind;
it is to the spirit what sleep is to the body,
nourishment and refreshment.

William Penn

Day 312

For what is faith
unless it is to believe
what you do not see?

St. Augustine

It is not what you say, or wish, or hope or intend,
it is only what you do that counts.

Brian Tracy

DAY 313

To argue against self reliance,
personal initiative and individual success
is to take the easy way, the road most traveled.

Tommy Newberry

No matter what you do, do it to your utmost…
I always attribute my success…
to always requiring myself to do my level best,
if only in driving a tack in straight.

Russell Conwell

DAY 314

If the axe is dull,
and one does not
sharpen the edge,
Then he must use more strength;
But wisdom brings success.

Ecclesiastes 10:10

A plan for each work hour of the day
solves not only the problems of each hour,
but also the problems of the whole of life.

Paul J. Meyer

> When you hire people
> that are smarter than you are,
> you prove you are smarter than they are.
>
> *R.H. Grant*

Day 315

> We always have time enough,
> if we will but use it aright.
>
> *Goethe*

Day 316

> This is the true joy in life,
> the being used for a purpose recognized by
> yourself as a mighty one;
> the being thoroughly worn out before
> you are thrown on the scrap heap;
> the being a force of nature instead
> of a feverish selfish little clod of ailments
> and grievances complaining that the world will
> not devote itself to making you happy.
>
> *George Bernard Shaw*

If you want to be a millionaire,
you must first become a million dollar person.

Tommy Newberry

Lord, make me an instrument of Your peace.
Where there is hatred let me sow love;
where there is injury, pardon;
where there is doubt, faith;
where there is despair, hope;
where there is darkness, light;
and where there is sadness, joy.

St. Francis of Assisi

DAY 317

Highly motivated achievers
are looking not to receive, but to contribute.
They are looking for problems
that are personally satisfying to solve.

Denis Waitley

If we really want to live,
we'd better start at once to try;
If we don't
it doesn't matter,
we'd better start to die.

W.H. Auden

DAY 318

If you fail to plan, you're planning to fail.

Robert Schuller

Day 319

All significant battles
are waged within the self.

Dan Millman

For as he thinks, in his heart, so is he.

Proverbs 23:7

Day 320

Life is a two for one deal.
With every choice,
you get a free consequence.

Tommy Newberry

I do not think that winning
is the most important thing.
I think it is the only thing.

Bill Veeck

DAY 321

Bad habits are easy to form,
but hard to live with;
good habits are hard to form,
but easy to live with.

A workout is 25% perspiration
and 75% inspiration.
Stated another way, it is one part exertion
and three parts discipline.
Doing it is easy once you get started.

George Allen

DAY 322

Day 323

The block of granite which was an obstacle
in the pathway of the weak
becomes a stepping-stone
in the pathway of the strong.

Thomas Carlyle

Chance favors the prepared mind.

Louis Pasteur

Day 324

Whatever your hand finds to do,
do it with all your might.

Ecclesiastes 9:10

Anyone who has done much counseling
will attest to the fact that those
who are successful in any field
are the goal setters.

Larry Burkette

The best way to know God
is to love many things.

Vincent van Gogh

He who controls others may be powerful,
but he who has mastered himself is mightier still.

Lao-Tzu

DAY 325

If a man knows not what harbor he seeks,
any wind is the right wind.

Lucius Annaeus Seneca

He conquers who endures.

DAY 326

Day 327

Anxiety and worry tend to vanish
into thin air when
you remind yourself
of all the blessings you possess.

Tommy Newberry

I shut my eyes in order to see.

Paul Gauguin

Day 328

Do not wait; the time will never be just right.
Start where you stand, and work with
whatever tools you may have at your command,
and better tools will be found as you go along.

Napoleon Hill

The important thing in life
is not the triumph
but the struggle;
the essential thing is not to have conquered
but to have fought well.

Day 329

Associate with men of good quality if you
esteem your own reputation;
for it is better to be alone than in bad company.

George Washington

Do not be fooled:
"Bad friends will ruin good habits."

1 Corinthians 15:33

Day 330

To know what is right
and not do it is the worst cowardice.

Confucius

You can either take action,
or you can hang back and hope for a miracle.
Miracles are great,
but they are so unpredictable.

Peter Drucker

DAY 331

Successful people have successful habits.
Mediocre people have mediocre habits.
And it all starts with a choice.

Tommy Newberry

Anyone can hold the helm
when the sea is calm.

DAY 332

Life is too short to be little.

Benjamin Disraeli

Never put off 'til tomorrow
what you can get someone else to do today!

Tommy Newberry

Rather fail with honor
than succeed by fraud.

Sophocles

DAY 333

Do what you can,
with what you have,
where you are.

Theodore Roosevelt

The entrepreneur is essentially a visualizer and
an actualizer...
He can visualize something,
and when he visualizes it he sees exactly
how to make it happen.

Robert L. Schwartz

DAY 334

We find only the world we look for.

Henry David Thoreau

> Image creates desire.
> You will what you imagine.
>
> *J.G. Gallimore*

Day 335

> Freedom is man's capacity to take a hand in his own development.
> It is our capacity to mold ourselves.

> Shallow men believe in luck.
> Strong men believe in cause and effect.
>
> *Ralph Waldo Emerson*

Day 336

> Whenever we're afraid,
> it's because we don't know enough.
> If we understood enough,
> we would never be afraid.
>
> *Earl Nightingale*

DAY 337

I do not think there is any other
quality so essential
to success of any kind
as the quality of perseverance.
It overcomes almost everything, even nature.

John D. Rockefeller

What's important is that
one strives to achieve a goal.

Ronald Reagan

DAY 338

Dare to be what your best self
knows you ought to be;
dare to be a bigger human being
than you have ever been.

Norman Vincent Peale

Habit is a cable;
we weave a thread of it each day,
and at last we cannot break it.

Horace Mann

Our greatest glory is not in never falling,
but in rising every time we fall.

Confucius

Day 339

If you employed study, thinking,
and planning time daily,
you could develop and use the power that can
change the course of your destiny.

W. Clement Stone

Success...seems to be connected with action.
Successful men keep moving.
They make mistakes, but they don't quit.

Conrad Hilton

Day 340

I know of no great men
except those who have rendered
great services to the human race.

Voltaire

It's the constant and determined effort
that breaks down all resistance,
sweeps away all obstacles.

Claude M. Bristol

DAY 341

Freedom is not only the right to succeed; it's the
right to fail...and then learn to succeed.
I have an equal opportunity to become unequal.
I don't expect a guarantee for equal results.

If I get out there and work harder
than the guy next to me,
if I spend more time on the field,
if I spend more time in the office,
if I risk more in my business,
I should have the right to make more,
to succeed more, than the guy next to me
who's not willing to do those same things.
That means no matter what color, what religion,
I have the right to be better
and receive better results.

Burgess Owens

DAY 342

Day 343

Through some strange and powerful principle of "mental chemistry" which she has never divulged, Nature wraps up in the impulse of strong desire, "that something" which recognizes no such word as "impossible," and accepts no such reality as failure.

Napoleon Hill

Worry is interest paid on trouble before it is due.

Day 344

You must believe that God never closes a door without opening another one.

Tommy Newberry

Nothing is particularly hard if you divide it into small jobs.

Henry Ford

366 Days of Wisdom & Inspiration

Day 345

Don't Quit

When things go wrong, as they sometimes will,
When the road you're trudging seems all uphill,
When the funds are low and the debts are high,
And you want to smile but you have to sigh,
When care is pressing you down a bit
Rest if you must, but just don't quit.

For life is queer with its twists and turns,
As every one of us sometimes learns,
And many a failure turns about,
When he might have won if he'd stuck it out.

Success is failure turned inside out,
The silver tint of the clouds of doubt,
And you never can tell how close you are,
It may be near when it seems so far.

So stick to the fight when you're hardest hit,
It's when things seem worse,
That you must not quit.

Day 346

We have forty million reasons for failure,
but not a single excuse.

Rudyard Kipling

Day 347

Whatever you vividly imagine,
ardently desire, sincerely believe,
and enthusiastically act upon
must inevitably come to pass.

Paul J. Meyer

A man carries his success or
his failure with him...
it does not depend on outside conditions.

Ralph Waldo Emerson

Day 348

God plus goals plus you
is an unbeatable combination!

Tommy Newberry

You cannot discover new oceans
unless you have the courage
to lose sight of the shore.

If you think like the masses you
will never dine with the classes.

Tommy Newberry

Day 349

It isn't always necessary to say words
when you pray.
Spend a minute just thinking about God.
Think how good He is, how kindly,
and that He is right by your side
guiding you and watching over you.

Norman Vincent Peale

Courage is resistance to fear,
mastery of fear... not absence of fear.

Mark Twain

Day 350

Never miss an opportunity
to make others happy,
even if you have to let them alone to do it.

Day 351

With every burning desire
comes the power to make it happen.
How hard and smart you're willing to work
is completely up to you.

Tommy Newberry

The secret of success
is constancy to purpose.

Benjamin Disraeli

Day 352

A workout makes you better today
than you were yesterday.
It strengthens the body,
relaxes the mind, toughens the spirit.
When you workout regularly,
your problems diminish
and your confidence grows.

George Allen

Day 353

Faith is like a boomerang;
begin using what you have
and it comes back
to you in greater measure.

Charles Allen

The imagination may be
compared to Adam's dream –
he awoke and found it truth.

John Keats

Day 354

Some things are within our control,
and some things are not.
It is only after you have faced up to this
fundamental rule and learned to distinguish
between what you can and can't control
that inner tranquillity and outer effectiveness
become possible.

Epictetus

Day 355

You are a product of your environment.
So choose the environment that will
best develop you toward your objective.
Analyze your life in terms of its environment.
Are the things around you helping you toward
success – or are they holding you back?

W. Clement Stone

Day 356

Curiosity is one of the permanent and certain
characteristics of a vigorous intellect.

Samuel Johnson

It's good to be just plain happy;
it's a little better to know that you're happy;
but to understand that you're happy
and to know why and how and still be happy,
be happy in the being and the knowing,
well that is beyond happiness, that is bliss.

Henry Miller

Day 357

Before arising each morning, voice
this affirmation:
"I believe, I believe, I believe."
then arise and believe your way through the day.

Norman Vincent Peale

Relentless, repetitive self talk
is what changes our self image.

Denis Waitley

Day 358

The principal part of faith is patience.

George MacDonald

Life responds to deserve and not to need.
It doesn't say, "If you need you will reap."
It says, "If you plant you will reap."
The guy says, "I really need to reap."
Then you really need to plant.

Jim Rohn

Day 359

A workout is a key
that helps unlock the door
of opportunity and success.
Hidden within each of us
is an extraordinary force.
Physical and mental fitness
are the triggers that can release it.

George Allen

Day 360

Faith is not a shelter against difficulties,
but belief in the face of all contradictions.

Paul Tournier

The great end of life is
not knowledge but action.

Thomas Henry Huxley

Day 361

Success is not a pie
with a limited number of pieces.
The success of others
has very little bearing on your success.
You and everyone you know can
become successful without anyone suffering
setbacks, harm, or downturns.

Denis Waitley

First you work on your goals,
then your goals work on you!

Tommy Newberry

Day 362

The plans of the diligent lead
surely to plenty.

Proverbs 21:5

Today will take its place as a single tile
in the mosaic of our finished lives –
to either add to its beauty and harmony
or detract from it in an
undedicated, purposeless life.

Earl Nightingale

A workout is a form of rebirth.
When you finish a good workout, you don't simply feel better,
you feel better about yourself.

George Allen

Day 363

Most of the evils in life
arise from man's being
unable to sit still in a room.

Blaise Pascal

Obstacles will look large or small to you
according to whether you are large or small.

Orison Swett Marden

Day 364

There is only one you.
God wanted you to be you.
Don't you dare change
just because you're outnumbered!

Charles Swindoll

Men are disturbed not by things,
but by the view which they take of them.

Epictetus

Build it and they will come!

Field of Dreams

DAY 365

Practice creative listening .
Get quiet so that insights
can come through your mind.

Norman Vincent Peale

Your success blesses others!

Tommy Newberry

DAY 366